The Sneezing Toucan

Written by Jim Munroe

Illustrated by Samantha Bell

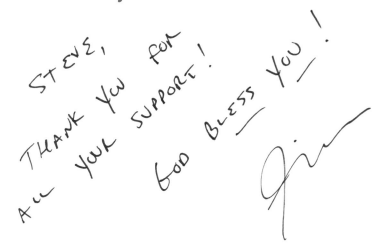

Steve,
Thank you for all your support!
God bless you!
Jim

Parson's Porch Books

The Sneezing Toucan

ISBN: Softcover 978-1-951472-94-8

Copyright © 2021 by Jim Munroe

Parson's Porch Books is an imprint of Parson's Porch *&* Company (PP*&*C) in Cleveland, Tennessee. PP*&*C is an innovative organization which raises money by publishing books of noted authors, representing all genres. Its face and voice is **David Russell Tullock** (dtullock@parsonsporch.com).

Another Saturday morning and I was riding my bike
Headed to town with my hair in a spike.
I really wanted to find just the right pet
And hoping my mom would not get upset.

She doesn't like snakes or lizards or cats
Or hamsters or pigs, no nothing like that.
No dogs, fish or turtles and no rabbits of course
And I'd better not think of ever getting a horse!

I thought about monkeys
and baby goats too
And I'm certain a chicken just
wouldn't do.
So into the shop I went
looking around
Wondering if the right pet
would ever be found.

Two puppies were wrestling:
a shepherd and collie.
There in the tank swam a
whole school of mollies.
Three Siamese kittens
in a box on the floor
And gerbils and ferrets
scurried all through the store!

A seven-foot python slithered in a large crate,
Although mom wouldn't like it, I thought he was great.
Then I noticed a cage sitting way in the back,
Inside stood a bird whose feathers were black.

His neck a bright yellow, his feet a pale blue,
His nose painted orange, and red and green too.
"What a beautiful bird!" I said to myself,
"I wonder why he's back here on the shelf."

While I stood there just staring at
the gorgeous toucan,
I felt a tap on my shoulder from the
old pet store man.
He said "Son, you don't want that
big-nosed black bird
Because he's got a problem
that's really absurd.

"In fact, he does something that
you just won't believe,
That big-nosed black bird can do
nothing but sneeze!"
Well, I stood there a moment
not sure what to do,
When all of a sudden that bird went
AAAchooo!

The man checked his watch; it was a
second past ten.
He said "In one hour, he will
do it again.
Hour by hour that bird just won't stop,
So I placed him here in the
back of the shop.

I've tried every cure from far
and from near
But he keeps right on sneezing,
it's been over two years!
Bottles and bottles of pills
big and small,
And as far as concoctions, well
I've tried them all."

That man rambled on for
30 minutes I bet,
About potions and lotions
and trips to the vet.
Well I thought and I
thought and then asked
the old man,
"How much do you want
for that sneezing
toucan?"

"He's been here a long time so
I'll sell him half price
And the cage will be free, but
take my advice.
At night you will want an
earplug or two,
And when he had said that,
the bird went

I glanced at the clock that hung over my head,
Just after eleven is what the hands read.
So I paid for the bird, tied the cage to the bike,
And hoping a toucan was something Mom likes.

As I pedaled home my stomach started to flip
And my knuckles turned white from a
very tight grip.
I walked in the kitchen, set the   cage
on a chair
And Mom stopped in her tracks
and started to stare.

"Well, I got him half price and just look at that beak! With all of those colors, he sure is unique! He's got one small problem and it's not a disease So don't be surprised when you hear his big sneeze."

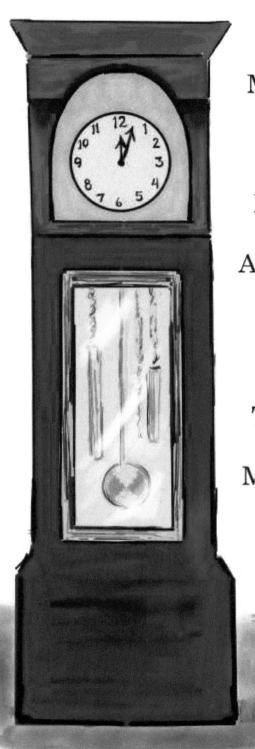

Mom said, "Yes that toucan is one gorgeous bird
But I'm not convinced it's a pet I prefer.
But I will be fair and I'll give you three days
And if he can quit sneezing then I'll let him stay."

The grandfather clock started chiming a tune,
The toucan sneezed loudly; it was just after noon.
Mom said "Hearing him sneeze can be quite a shock
But it's still not as loud as those bongs from the clock."

Day Number Two and I needed a plan
So I put fruit and veggies inside a large pan.
I fed him at breakfast and I fed him at lunch,
All through the day he continued to munch.

The toucan ate cherries and carrots and beans,
And apples and corn and two tangerines.
I tried melons and grapes and celery and peas,
But that bird like a clock just
continued to sneeze.

As I crawled into bed
I heard my mom say,
"If he still sneezes tomorrow
you know he can't stay.
I must leave in the morning;
I'll be back after noon,
You'd better think of a cure
and it'd better be soon."

The next morning came fast
and I heard the loud chimes,
That toucan sneezed hard at a
second past nine.

Then I got an idea that I
thought might succeed!
So I grabbed all the tools
that I thought I would need.

I found the brass key,
slid it into the lock
And removed every chime
from the grandfather clock!

I made a shelf for the cage, the toucan looked great,
Then removed the glass door
as Mom came through the gate.

She came through the hallway
and looked at the bird
And her mouth opened wide
but did not say a word.
"Well, the bongs were much
louder compared to his sneeze
So I took out the chimes and I
thought you'd be pleased."

Then her face began melting and she said
with a smile,
"Well it looks like that bird can stay quite awhile.
Now our clock is unique and the toucan is too."
It was a tick after one and all we heard was AAA...

...chooo!

CPSIA information can be obtained
at www.ICGtesting.com
Printed in the USA
JSHW032351250421
13973JS00001B/1